Challenger Writing
SECOND EDITION
ADULT READING SERIES

Skill-building writing exercises
for each lesson in *Challenger 7* of the
Challenger Adult Reading Series

Practical Strategies, Inc.

New Readers Press

Writing for Challenger 7, 2nd Edition
ISBN 978-1-56420-906-1

Copyright © 2010 New Readers Press
New Readers Press
ProLiteracy's Publishing Division
104 Marcellus Street, Syracuse, NY 13204
www.newreaderspress.com

All rights reserved. No part of this book may be reproduced or transmitted in any form or by any means, electronic or mechanical, including photocopying, recording, or by any information storage and retrieval system, without permission in writing from the publisher.

Printed in the United States of America
9 8 7 6 5

Proceeds from the sale of New Readers Press materials support professional development, training, and technical assistance programs of ProLiteracy that benefit local literacy programs in the U.S. and around the globe.

Developmental Editor: Terrie Lipke
Contributing Editor: Terry Ledyard
Contributing Writer: Practical Strategies, Inc.
Creative Director: Andrea Woodbury
Cover Design: Carolyn Wallace

Contents

Lesson 1 4

Lesson 2 6

Lesson 3 8

Lesson 4 10

Lesson 5 12

Lesson 6 14

Lesson 7 16

Lesson 8 18

Lesson 9 20

Lesson 10 22

Lesson 11 24

Lesson 12 26

Lesson 13 28

Lesson 14 30

Lesson 15 32

Lesson 16 34

Lesson 17 36

Lesson 18 38

Lesson 19 40

Lesson 20 42

Review 44

Lesson 1

1 Choose the Best Descriptive Words and Phrases. On the lines below on the left, write three descriptive words and phrases from the story "Storm at Sea." Choose the ones that you think are the best. On the lines to the right of each word or phrase, tell why you think it is a good description.

> Details are words and phrases that add specific information to describe a person, place, or thing. *Descriptive words and phrases* are special kinds of details.
>
> - Some descriptions tell how a person, place, or thing looks, smells, tastes, sounds, and feels such as *hot sun*. Other examples are *pale pink* for look, *fresh* for smell, *sour* for taste, and *loud* for sound. These are vivid words.
> - Specific words name people, places, and things, for example, the writer names the city, New York, instead of writing "the city." Give as much detail as you can. Instead of writing *store*, tell the kind of store. (Examples: shoe store, supermarket, bodega)
> - Another way to make details more interesting is to use action verbs. Instead of writing "she said," try an action word such as *stated, informed, yelled, reported, declared, cautioned,* or *whispered.*
>
> Using descriptive words and phrases tells more and makes your writing more interesting.

1. _____ _____

2. _____ _____

3. _____ _____

2 Add Details. Choose details from the list to make each sentence more interesting and tell more about the topic of the sentence. You may need to change words or add words.

| little | Maggie's | his | sister | grim | and upset |

1. Kyle was worried over the news.

| calm | screaming | circling | slowly moving | seagulls |

2. Kyle watched the sea and the birds over the ship.
   _____

| three | deadly | mom | depressed | angry |

3. Years ago there had been a car accident.
   _____

3 What Will You Write About? In Exercise 4, you will write a three-paragraph summary of the story "Storm at Sea."

> A summary is much shorter than an actual article or story. For a summary, you need only the most important points and their details. To find the most important points of a story, ask yourself the "Five W's and H" questions.

1. Who are the characters in the story? _____
2. What is the action in the story? _____
   _____
3. Where does the story take place? _____
4. When does it take place? _____
5. Why is this action taking place? _____
6. How does the story end? _____
   _____

4 Write a Three-Paragraph Summary. On a separate sheet of paper, write a three-paragraph summary of the story "Storm at Sea."

When you write, remember to:

1. Prewrite: Reread the answers to the "Five W's and H" questions, and add details that you think will help to make your summary clear.

2. Paragraph 1, Introduction: Tell what you are going to write about. This is your topic sentence, or the main idea, of the summary. Make it your first sentence. Include the title and the author of the story in your introduction.

3. Paragraph 2, Body: Use the answers to the "Five W's and H" questions to develop your summary. Remember to use details to add interest to your summary.

4. Paragraph 3, Conclusion: Tell what you wrote about, but use different words. You might end your summary with a question such as "Was Kyle right in taking the money?" or "Was Salama really a friend if Kyle gets in trouble?"

Lesson 2

1 Choose the Best Descriptive Words and Phrases. On the lines below on the left, write three descriptive words and phrases from the story "The Good Lord Will Provide." Choose the ones that you think are the best. On the lines to the right of each word or phrase, tell why you think it is a good description.

1. _____   _____
   _____

2. _____   _____
   _____

3. _____   _____
   _____

2 Add Details. Read the sentences below. Then rewrite them so they are more interesting and clear. The first one is done for you.

> Besides describing a person, place, thing, or idea, details can also explain how something is done. Sometimes adding just a few words is enough. Other times you need to add whole sentences to make your writing more interesting and clear. Which of the two sets of sentences below tells you more?
>
> ...I told the city fellas I was a good driver....
>
> ...I told the city fellas that I could just about drive a car up one side of a wall and down the other side....

1. Plastering the wall was messy.
   Plastering the cracked bedroom wall was a messy job, and I got plaster in my hair.

2. I got stuck in a blizzard.
   _____
   _____

3. The child wore a blazer.
   _____
   _____

4. I was late for work.

_____

_____

3 What Will You Write About? In Exercise 4, you will write a three-paragraph expository essay to answer the question: What is the trick that Walt plays on the sheriff and the deputies? Mapping the story will help you gather information for your essay. If you need more room, copy the map below onto a separate sheet of paper.

Trick:

Why is Walt in prison?	Why does Judy need the south field plowed?	How does Walt get the sheriff to dig up the field?

4 Write a Three-Paragraph Expository Essay. On a separate sheet of paper, write a three-paragraph expository essay to answer the question: What is the trick that Walt plays on the sheriff and the deputies?

> An expository essay is one that explains information. It may explain how to do something, how two things are the same or different, or how one thing causes something else to happen. In this essay, you are going to explain how Walt's letter caused the sheriff to dig up the south field.

When you write, remember to:

1. Prewrite: First, think about what you are going to write. Reread the map of the story. Draw lines vertically below each box to add details if you think you will need more information.

2. Paragraph 1: Write an introductory paragraph. Tell what you are going to write about. This is your topic sentence. In this paragraph, you should also explain that the story is really letters back and forth between a husband and wife.

3. Paragraph 2: Use the information from the map to tell how Walt tricked the sheriff. Be sure you have enough details so that your reader will understand the trick.

4. Paragraph 3: Use different words to tell what you wrote about. You might end your essay by saying what you think about the trick, or what you thought when you read the last letter from Walt.

Lesson 3

1 Choose the Best Descriptive Words and Phrases. On the lines below on the left, write three descriptive words and phrases from the story "Mr. Manning's Money Tree: Part I." Choose the ones that you think are the best. On the lines to the right of each word or phrase, tell why you think it is a good description.

1. _____   _____
   _____

2. _____   _____
   _____

3. _____   _____
   _____

2 Try Your Hand at Using Details. Write a sentence to describe each idea below from the story "Mr. Manning's Money Tree: Part I." Use details to make each sentence as interesting, complete, and clear as possible.

1. why Henry Manning stole $30,000

2. planting the spruce

3. hiding the thermos

4. how Henry felt when he realized that he couldn't dig up the spruce

3 What Will You Write About? In Exercise 4, you will write a three-paragraph summary of "Mr. Manning's Money Tree: Part I." To help you gather and organize information for the summary, answer the "Five W's and H" questions.

1. Who are the characters in the story? _____

2. What is the action in the story? _____
   _____
   _____

3. Where does the story take place? _____

4. When does it take place? _____

5. Why is this action taking place? _____
   _____

6. How does Part I end? _____
   _____

4 Write a Three-Paragraph Summary. On a separate sheet of paper, write a three-paragraph summary of "Mr. Manning's Money Tree: Part I."

When you write, remember to:

1. Prewrite: Reread the answers to the "Five W's and H" questions, and add details that you think will help make your summary clear and complete. But remember: a summary uses only the most important points.

2. Paragraph 1, Introduction: Tell what you are going to write about. This is your topic sentence, or the main idea, of the summary. Make it your first sentence. Because you are writing about a story, include the title and the author in your introduction.

3. Paragraph 2, Body: Use the answers to the "Five W's and H" questions to develop your summary. Use details to make the idea clear and complete.

4. Paragraph 3, Conclusion: Tell what you wrote about, but use different words. You might end with a sentence such as "I wonder what happens next" or "Will Henry's plan work?"

Lesson 4

1 Choose the Best Descriptive Words and Phrases. On the lines below on the left, write three descriptive words and phrases from the story "Mr. Manning's Money Tree: Part II." Choose the ones that you think are the best. On the lines to the right of each word or phrase, tell why you think it is a good description.

1. _____ _____
   _____

2. _____ _____
   _____

3. _____ _____
   _____

2 Add Transitions. Write a number from 1 through 6 next to each sentence below to show the correct time order in which the things happen in the story. Then use at least three of the transitions listed in the box to make the order clear. Mark the changes to the sentences below.

> In retelling how something happened, it is important to tell it in the order in which it happened. Transitions connect one idea to another and make the order easier to understand. *First, second, third,* etc., are transitions. Other transitions that show time order are *after, after a while, afterward, at last, at once, before, during, finally, last, later, next, now, right away, soon,* and *then.*
>
> **After** serving his time, Henry left prison. **Finally,** he was going to dig up his money.

_____ Henry proposes to Constance.

_____ Jerome Smith writes to Constance that he wants a divorce.

_____ Henry starts to visit Constance without the excuse of taking care of her car.

_____ Henry becomes the successful owner of the garage and an auto dealership.

_____ Henry hatches a plan to become friendly with the Smiths.

_____ Henry strikes up a friendship with Constance Smith.

3 What Will You Write About? In Exercise 4, you will write a three-paragraph expository essay to answer the question: What kind of a person is Henry?

- First, list below at least six personality traits, or characteristics, that describe Henry.

1. _____   3. _____   5. _____

2. _____   4. _____   6. _____

- Then choose the three traits that you think best describe Henry—and that you can most easily explain.

- If you need more room, copy the following table onto a separate sheet of paper. Write details for each characteristic that you chose.

Personality Traits	Details
1.	1. 2.
2.	1. 2.
3.	1. 2.

4 Write a Three-Paragraph Expository Essay. On a separate sheet of paper, write a three-paragraph expository essay to answer the question: What kind of a person is Henry?

When you write, remember to:

1. Prewrite: Reread your list of personality traits and details. Make sure that these are the traits and details that you want to use. Now is the time to change your mind and revise your ideas.

2. Paragraph 1, Introduction: Tell what you are going to write about. This is your topic sentence. List the three personality traits, but don't give any details yet. Include the title of the story and the author. Point out that Henry is the main character in the story.

3. Paragraph 2, Body: Develop the information about Henry. Depending on how you organize it, you might be able to use transitions that show time order. For example, you might say "Finally, Henry realizes that he never needed the money under the tree."

4. Conclusion: Retell what you wrote about, but in different words. You might sum up your ideas with an ending to your essay like "Would Henry have been different if he had not gone back for the money? I hope not because this Henry is a good guy."

Lesson 4   11

Lesson 5

1 Choose the Best Descriptive Words and Phrases. On the lines below on the left, write three descriptive words and phrases from the story "All the Years of Her Life." Choose the ones that you think are the best. On the lines to the right of each word or phrase, tell why you think it is a good description.

1. _____   _____
   _____

2. _____   _____
   _____

3. _____   _____
   _____

2 Add Transitions. Write a number from 1 through 8 next to each sentence below to show the correct time order in which the things happen in the story. Then use at least three of the transitions listed in the box on page 10 to make the order clear. Mark the changes to the sentences below.

_____ Mrs. Higgins pours herself a cup of tea and sighs.

_____ Mr. Carr respects Mrs. Higgins's quiet dignity and goodness.

_____ Alfred has to empty his pockets.

_____ Mrs. Higgins asks Mr. Carr what has happened.

_____ Alfred feels like he has never really seen his mother before.

_____ Mr. Carr tells Alfred he is going to turn him over to the police.

_____ Mrs. Higgins walks fast and won't let Alfred talk.

_____ Mrs. Higgins explains that sometimes it takes a while for people to grow up.

3 What Will You Write About? In Exercise 4, you will write a summary of the story "All the Years of Her Life." Use the "Five W's and H" questions to gather information about the story. Remember that a summary hits on just the main points.

1. Who are the characters in the story? _____

2. What action takes place in the story? _____
   _____
   _____

3. When does the story take place? _____

4. Where does the story take place? _____

5. Why does the action take place? _____
   _____
   _____

6. How does the story end? _____
   _____

4 Write a Three-Paragraph Summary. On a separate sheet of paper, write a three-paragraph summary of the story "All the Years of Her Life."

When you write, remember to:

1. Prewrite: Reread the answers to the "Five W's and H" questions. Ask yourself if you have the main points of the story.

2. Paragraph 1, Introduction: Tell what you are going to write about. Make it your topic sentence. Because it is a summary, give the title and author of the story.

3. Paragraph 2, Body: Build the body of the summary by explaining the main points of the story. You don't need a lot of details, but you need enough to make what happens in the story clear.

4. Paragraph 3, Conclusion: Restate what you wrote about. Because this is a summary, you don't include your own opinions about the characters or what happened.

Lesson 6

1 Choose the Best Descriptive Words and Phrases. On the lines below on the left, write three descriptive words and phrases from the story "Prelude." Choose the ones that you think are the best. On the lines to the right of each word or phrase, tell why you think it is a good description.

1. _____   _____
   _____

2. _____   _____
   _____

3. _____   _____
   _____

2 Add Transitions. Revise the sentences below to add transitions that add information.

> Some transitions can be used to add information and connect ideas between sentences. By using these transitions, your ideas flow more smoothly from sentence to sentence. Some transitions that add information are *along with, also, another, as well as, besides, finally, for example, in addition, last, next,* and position words like *first, second, third,* etc.
>
> Harry and Mr. Silverstein were hurt. *In addition,* the newsstand was destroyed.

1. People were willing to watch, but not to help. No one called the police.
   _____
   _____

2. The gang members attacked Harry. They knocked over the newsstand.
   _____
   _____

3. The story says a lot about people. People in a crowd do what the crowd does. People put their own safety ahead of helping anyone else.
   _____
   _____

3 What Will You Write About? In Exercise 4, you will write an essay to answer the following question: Why do you think that no one helps the Silversteins? Use your own knowledge and experience to answer the question. Brainstorming will help you gather ideas.

> When you brainstorm, you write down everything that comes to mind about a topic. You don't think about the ideas as you write them. If you did, you might decide that some aren't good and cross them out. Those might turn out to be the best ideas, so just write as many ideas as you can. The more you list, the more you will have to choose from when you plan your writing. Use a separate sheet of paper if you need more space.

1. _____   3. _____
2. _____   4. _____

- Then choose the three reasons that you think best describe why people don't help the Silversteins—and that you can most easily explain.
- On a separate sheet of paper, copy the following table and write details for each reason.

Reasons People Don't Help the Silversteins	Details
1.	1. 2.

4 Write a Three-Paragraph Expository Essay. On a separate sheet of paper, write a three-paragraph expository essay to answer this question: Why do you think that no one helps the Silversteins? Use your own knowledge and experience to answer the question.

When you write, remember to:

1. Prewrite: Reread the three reasons that you chose and the details that you listed for each. Are you satisfied that these are good reasons and that you can explain them? Now is the time to change what you want to write about—not after you've started writing.

2. Paragraph 1, Introduction: Tell what you are going to write about. This is your topic sentence. Include the author and title of the story. In two or three sentences, summarize what happens to the Silversteins. You don't need to summarize the whole story, just the attack and the crowd.

3. Paragraph 2, Body: Write one sentence for your first reason. Add a sentence or two to explain it. Then begin the sentence that introduces reason 2 with a transition that adds information. Write a couple of sentences to explain reason 2. Then add reason 3, also beginning with a transition that adds information.

4. Paragraph 3, Conclusion: Tell what you wrote about, but in different words. State the three reasons again. End with your opinion about coming to the aid of someone in need.

Lesson 7

1 Try Your Hand at Using Details. List at least three words or phrases to describe each character in the story "The Test."

1. Marian: _____

2. Mrs. Ericson: _____

3. the inspector: _____

2 Add Transitions. Revise the sentences below to add transitions that show causes or effects.

> A cause is an action that makes something else happen. That something else is called an effect. Certain transitions can help you connect causes with their effects: *as a result, because, because of, consequently, on account of, so,* and *then.*
>
> Did Marian fail her test **because** she was a bad driver?

1. Mrs. Ericson got out of the car. The inspector felt he could insult Marian.

2. The inspector was mean to Marian. First, she was African American. Second, she was a woman.

3. Marian failed the test. She would not be able to pick up the children after school.

3 What Will You Write About? In Exercise 4, you will write a three-paragraph expository essay to answer this question: Why do you think that people are prejudiced?

- To help you answer this question, brainstorm at least four ideas. Write them on the lines below.

1. _____   3. _____

2. _____   4. _____

- Circle the three ideas that you think you can develop into a good essay.

- Fill in details for each idea. If you need more room, copy the following table onto a separate sheet of paper.

Ideas/Reasons	Details
1.	1. 2. 3.
2.	1. 2. 3.
3.	1. 2. 3.

4 Write a Three-Paragraph Expository Essay. On a separate sheet of paper, write a three-paragraph expository essay to answer this question: Why do you think that people are prejudiced?

When you write, remember to:

1. Prewrite: Review your table. Now that you have listed details for your three ideas, do you still want to write about them? Now is the time to change your plan. Do you have enough details to explain your ideas completely?

2. Paragraph 1, Introduction: In a topic sentence, tell what you are going to write about. In one or two sentences, tell why you have this opinion. That is, state your ideas, but don't write any details.

3. Paragraph 2, Body: Develop your three ideas. Use details to explain each one. Use transitions that show cause and effect to connect details to your ideas.

4. Paragraph 3, Conclusion: Restate your opinion and the reasons that support your opinion. Use different words. You might end with some sentences about how prejudice might be stopped.

Lesson 8

1 Try Your Hand at Using Details. List words and phrases that describe these characters from the story "Charles." Then write one sentence for each character, and use as many details from your list as you can.

1. Charles:

2. Laurie:

3. Charles:

4. Laurie:

2 Add Transitions. Add transitions that compare and contrast information. Write the new sentences on the lines below.

> To compare means to look for the ways that people, places, or things are the same. To contrast means to look for the ways that people, places, or things are different. Transitions that show similarities and differences include:
>
> Comparison: *as well as, both, in common, in comparison, like, same, similar, too*
>
> Differences: *although, but, however, in contrast, instead, on the other hand, unlike, yet*

1. Laurie does bad things. He is not a bad child.

2. Laurie's father seems like a nice man. His mother seems like a nice person.

3. Charles the helper hands out crayons. The Charles who does bad things throws them.

3 What Will You Write About? In Exercise 4, you will write a three-paragraph expository essay to answer the question: How is Charles the helper different from Charles who does bad things? If you need more room, copy the chart onto a separate sheet of paper. Fill in each side of the chart with examples from the story.

> A T-chart is a good organizing and planning tool. It can help you list and identify how people or things are alike or different, and the advantages and disadvantages or the pros and cons of something.

Charles the Helper	Charles Who Does Bad Things

4 Write a Three-Paragraph Expository Essay. On a separate sheet of paper, write a three-paragraph essay to answer the question: How is Charles the helper different from Charles who does bad things?

When you write, remember to:

1. Prewrite: Review the T-chart. Do you have at least three differences between the two Charleses? If not, go back and add what you need. Three of anything—examples, ideas, or reasons—is usually a good number to use to support your topic.

2. Paragraph 1, Introduction: Tell what you are going to write about. Include the title of the story and the name of the author. List the three ways that the two Charleses are different, but don't give details.

3. Paragraph 2, Body: Explain how Charles the helper and Charles who does bad things are alike. Use at least two transitions to help you show the differences.

4. Paragraph 3, Conclusion: Tell what you wrote about. List the three differences without details. Then tie up the ideas with a closing sentence that tells what you think of the two Charleses.

5. Reread your essay. Check spelling and capitalization.

Lesson 9

1 Try Your Hand at Using Details. Write a sentence about each character listed below from the story "The Open Window." Use details from the story to make the sentences interesting, clear, and complete.

1. the niece: _____

   _____

2. Mrs. Sappleton: _____

   _____

3. Mr. Framton: _____

   _____

2 Combine the Sentences. Correct and combine each set of run-on sentences below.

> A run-on sentence is two or more complete ideas that run together. There is no word like *and* and a comma, or *although* and a comma, or a period to tell you where one idea ends and the other begins.
>
> The ending surprised me I had no idea what was coming.
>
> The ending surprised me **because** I had no idea what was coming.

1. I wonder what her aunt and uncle would say they knew what their niece was like.

   _____

   _____

2. Mr. Framton was an odd person anyway all he talked about was his illnesses Mrs. Sappleton said.

   _____

   _____

3. The spaniel was tired the men were covered in mud Mrs. Sappleton was happy to see them.

   _____

   _____

3 What Will You Write About? In Exercise 4, you will write a three-paragraph persuasive essay to answer the question: Was it wrong of the niece to make up a story to tell Mr. Framton? Why or why not?

> The goal of a persuasive essay is to get someone to agree with you or to do what you want that person to do. For this essay, you want your reader to agree with your opinion. You need to state clearly your reasons and base them on facts from the story and your own experience. This includes your values.

- Create a T-chart to list reasons why it was wrong to tell the story and reasons why it wasn't.

Wrong	Not Wrong

- Decide what you think based on your ideas: _____

4 Write a Three-Paragraph Persuasive Essay. On a separate sheet of paper, write a three-paragraph persuasive essay to answer the question: Was it wrong of the niece to make up a story to tell Mr. Framton? Why or why not?

When you write, remember to:

1. Prewrite: Reread your T-chart and be sure that this is the opinion that you want to write about. Also, be sure that you have at least three reasons to write about.

2. Introduction: Tell why you are writing this paragraph. This is your topic sentence, so make it the first sentence. Because this is a short story, include the title and author.

3. Body of the paragraph: Use the three reasons you chose to build the body of the paragraph. Write at least one sentence to explain each reason. Add details to make the reasons clear. Use the transitions *first, second,* and *third* as you add the reasons to the paragraph.

4. Conclusion: Restate what you wrote about, but use different words. Tie up your essay with a closing sentence. You might end with a question such as "How would you like to be Mr. Framton running for his life?"

5. Reread your essay. Check spelling and capitalization.

Lesson 10

1 Try Your Hand at Using Details. Write a sentence for each idea listed below based on the story "Down the Rabbit-Hole" (from *Alice in Wonderland*). Use details to make the sentences interesting, clear, and complete.

1. Alice:_____

2. what a tiny golden key might open: _____

3. how you would feel if you were Alice:_____

2 Combine the Sentences. Correct and combine each set of run-on sentences below.

> Because you are writing the sentences out by hand, underline the title of the book. If you were typing on a keyboard, you would use italics.

1. The story's writer had a vivid imagination *Alice in Wonderland* is a very unusual story.

2. Science fiction movies give me the creeps I have bad dreams after I see one.

3. I don't like fantasy I saw the Disney movie once it was good.

3 What Will You Write About? In Exercise 4, you will write a three-paragraph essay to explain an adventure that you once had. It can be a scary adventure or a fun one. If you can't think of an adventure, you can make one up. Use the "Five W's and H" questions to help you gather details for your essay.

1. Who was involved in the adventure? _____
2. What happened on the adventure? _____
   _____
   _____
3. When did the adventure take place? _____
4. Where did it take place? _____
5. Why did it take place? _____
   _____
6. How did you feel either while you were on the adventure or after it was over? _____
   _____
   _____

4 Write a Three-Paragraph Expository Essay. On a separate sheet of paper, write a three-paragraph essay to explain an adventure that you once had.

When you write, remember to:

1. Prewrite: Reread the answers to the "Five W's and H" questions and add details that you think will help to make your adventure clear and more complete for your reader.

2. Paragraph 1, Introduction: Make your first sentence your topic sentence. Include in this paragraph who was on the adventure and when it happened. This sets the scene for the body of the paragraph where you describe the adventure.

3. Paragraph 2, Body: Develop the body using the answers to the other questions, but save the answer to the "H" question for the conclusion. Use transitions that show time order or that add information to help your ideas flow.

4. Paragraph 3, Conclusion: Tell what you wrote about, but use different words. Use the answer to the "H" question to tie up your ideas in the essay. You might end with a sentence such as "I really enjoyed, . . ." or "Once I found out the truth, I laughed at how scared I was."

Lesson 11

1 Try Your Hand at Using Details. Write a sentence for each idea listed below from the story "Sleep Disorder." Use details to make the sentences interesting, clear, and complete.

1. "sleep like a log": _____
   _____

2. a nightmare: _____
   _____

3. a happy dream: _____
   _____

2 Combine the Sentences. Combine and correct each set of sentences and sentence fragments below.

> The verb is the action word in a sentence and tells what is happening. The subject tells who or what is acting. If the subject or verb is missing, it is a sentence fragment, not a sentence. Part of what makes a group of words into a sentence is missing.
>
> **Anika lying** on the bed.   **Anika is lying** on the bed.
> subject—no verb   subject—verb
>
> **Lay** on the bed.   **Anika lay** on the bed last night.
> verb—no subject   subject—verb
>
> There is one kind of sentence in which the subject is not stated, but is understood to be "you." That is a sentence that tells a person to do something.
>
> [you] Lie down on the bed.

1. Anika bored by her job. She wished for more excitement.
   _____
   _____

2. Difficult to tell what is real in the story what is not.
   _____
   _____

3. Anika dreaming she was the doctor or she really was the doctor.
   _____
   _____

3 What Will You Write About? In Exercise 4, you will write a three-paragraph essay explaining either what you think is real in the story or what you think is a dream.

- First, you need to decide what is real and what is a dream, so fill in a T-chart like the one below. Use a separate sheet of paper if you need more room.

What Is Real	What Is a Dream

- Second, circle the part—either what you think is real or what you think is a dream—that you want to write about.
- Third, list details from the story that support your opinion. Use a separate sheet of paper, and list at least six details you can use as reasons. Then choose the best three reasons.

4 Write a Three-Paragraph Expository Essay. On a separate sheet of paper, write a three-paragraph expository essay on the following topic: Choose either an event in the story that you think is real or one that you think is a dream. Explain the reasons for your opinion.

When you write, remember to:

1. Prewrite: Reread your list of reasons and be sure that you have the best examples to write about.
2. Introduction: Tell why you are writing this essay. This is your topic sentence, so make it the first sentence. Because you are writing about a short story, include the story's title.
3. Body of the paragraph: Use the three reasons you chose to build the body of the paragraph. Write at least one sentence to explain each reason. Add details to make the reasons clear. Use the transitions *first, second,* and *third* as you add the reasons to the paragraph.
4. Conclusion: Restate what you wrote about, but use different words. Tie up your essay with a closing sentence. You might end with a question such as "What do you think?" or a sentence such as "I found the story very difficult to understand."
5. Reread your essay. Check spelling and capitalization.

Lesson 12

1 Try Your Hand at Using Details. Write a sentence for each idea listed below from the story "The Boarded Window." Use details to make the sentence interesting, clear, and complete.

1. the most frightening thing that ever happened to me: _____
   _____
   _____

2. what I think about the story "The Boarded Window": _____
   _____
   _____

3. an old man with long white hair and beard: _____
   _____
   _____

2 Combine the Sentences. Correct and combine the following sentence fragments and sentences.

1. Died from a fever. Murlock didn't seem sorry.
   _____
   _____

2. Murlock awoke because of the noise. The panther dragging the body to the window.
   _____
   _____

3. She was dead. How a piece of the panther's ear in her teeth?
   _____
   _____

3 What Will You Write About? In Exercise 4, you will write a three-paragraph essay explaining what you think about this story. Did you like it or didn't you? Why?

- First, state your opinion.

My opinion of this story: _____

- Second, list examples to support your opinion.

1. _____
2. _____
3. _____
4. _____
5. _____
6. _____

4 Write a Three-Paragraph Expository Essay. On a separate sheet of paper, write a three-paragraph expository essay to answer the question: Did you like the story "The Boarded Window" or not? Why?

When you write, remember to:

1. Prewrite: Reread your opinion and your list of examples from the story. Choose the best three to write about. These are the best examples and the ones that you can explain most easily.

2. Introduction: Tell what you are writing about. This is your topic sentence, so make it the first sentence. Because this is a short story, include the title and author.

3. Body of the paragraph: Use the three reasons you chose to build the body of the paragraph. Write at least one sentence to explain each reason. Add details to make the reasons clear. Use transitions that add information, or show cause and effect to help you connect your ideas. Which type of transition you use depends on how you are explaining your ideas.

4. Conclusion: Restate what you wrote about, but use different words. Tie up your essay with a closing sentence such as "You can tell that I really didn't like this story," or "I thought this was a great, scary story."

5. Reread your essay. Check spelling and capitalization.

Lesson 13

1 Try Your Hand at Using Details. Write two sentences to describe each of the characters in this scene from the play "On Golden Pond."

1. Ethel: _____
   _____
   _____

2. Norman: _____
   _____
   _____

2 Combine the Sentences. Each set of sentences below has a problem with commas. Correct the comma fault by combining sentences.

> A common mistake in writing is to try combining sentences using only a comma. There are different ways to correct the problem. You can:
> - use a coordinating conjunction such as *and, but, or, nor, so, yet* and a comma to combine ideas.
> - use a subordinating conjunction such as *after, although, though, because, before, if, since,* and *when* and a comma to combine ideas.
> - use a relative pronoun such as *who, whom, which, whose,* and *that*.
>
>   Norman sits on the couch, Ethel runs to get the medicine.
>   Norman sits on the couch, **while** Ethel runs to get the medicine.

1. Norman frightens Ethel,she begins to yell at him.
   _____
   _____

2. Ethel wants to take her mother's china home with them,Norman decides to carry one of the boxes.
   _____
   _____

3. Ethel and Norman seem to joke with each other a lot, this makes the scene funny at times.
   _____
   _____

3 What Will You Write About? In Exercise 4, you will write a three-paragraph letter to persuade Norman that he must take it easy. Make believe that you are his son or daughter, or a friend. To help you gather information, organize, and plan your essay, brainstorm at least six reasons that he should take it easy. Write your ideas below.

1. _____
2. _____
3. _____
4. _____
5. _____
6. _____

4 Write a Three-Paragraph Persuasive Letter. On a separate sheet of paper, write a three-paragraph letter to persuade Norman that he must take it easy. Make believe that you are his son or daughter, or a friend.

When you write, remember to:

1. Prewrite: Reread your brainstormed list. Choose the three reasons that you think are the strongest and you can best explain.

2. Set up the format for a friendly letter: address, date, and greeting.

3. Paragraph 1, Introduction: Explain why you are writing the letter. This is your topic sentence, so make it the first. Add a few details such as you have heard that he hasn't been feeling well and recently had an angina attack. This sets up the reason for your letter.

4. Paragraph 2, Body: Develop your reasons that Norman should take it easy. Write at least one sentence to explain each reason. Use transitions that add information to help you connect the three reasons and their details.

5. Paragraph 3, Conclusion: Restate why you are writing the letter. Restate the three reasons, but without the details. End with a sentence that asks Norman to take your advice.

6. Add the closing and your signature.

7. Check spelling and capitalization.

Lesson 14

1 Try Your Hand at Using Details. Write two sentences to describe each of the following ideas from the reading "The Execution."

1. the Tzar: _____
   _____
   _____

2. the prisoner who went mad: _____
   _____
   _____

3. the priest: _____
   _____
   _____

2 Combine the Sentences. Each set of sentences below has a problem with commas. Correct the comma fault by combining sentences.

1. Fyodor was sentenced to death, he had opposed the Tzar.
   _____
   _____

2. The guards didn't seem to want to execute the prisoners, the guards seemed sorry to do their duty.
   _____
   _____

3. Fyodor was freed after four years, he never got over the experience, he was marked for life by it.
   _____
   _____

3 What Will You Write About? In Exercise 4, you will write a three-paragraph essay that answers the question: How do you think that Fyodor was changed by his near-death experience?

- To help you answer the question, first think of what you know about Fyodor at the time of the execution. List what you know.

1. _____   3. _____

2. _____   4. _____

- Now brainstorm at least six ideas about how Fyodor could have changed after the morning of the scheduled execution.

1. _____
2. _____
3. _____
4. _____
5. _____
6. _____

4 Write a Three-Paragraph Expository Essay. On a separate sheet of paper, write a three-paragraph essay that answers the question: How do you think that Fyodor was changed by his near-death experience?

When you write, remember to:

1. Prewrite: Review your list of what you know about Fyodor. Then review your list of how you think he changed. Do you think that your ideas are realistic? If so, choose the best three ideas to write about. If not, try brainstorming again.

2. Paragraph 1, Introduction: Begin with a topic sentence. Describe Fyodor on the morning of the execution.

3. Paragraph 2, Body: Describe how you think Fyodor changed as a result of his near-death experience. Use transitions that show cause and effect, that add information, or that compare and contrast.

4. Paragraph 3, Conclusion: Restate the topic of the essay. Restate how you think Fyodor changed. Tie up your ideas with a sentence such as "I can't imagine the fear that Fyodor felt that morning," or "After that, who wouldn't change."

5. Check spelling and capitalization.

Lesson 15

1 Try Your Hand at Using Details. Write two sentences about each idea from the story "A Day's Wait" listed below.

1. having a headache: _____
   _____
   _____

2. having the flu: _____
   _____
   _____

3. taking medicine according to instructions: _____
   _____
   _____

2 Combine the Sentences. Correct the comma faults, run-on sentences, and sentence fragments in the sentences below by combining them.

1. Schatz feeling sick. His father called the doctor, he came right away.
   _____
   _____

2. Schatz didn't understand, the thermometer used in France is different from the one used here.
   _____
   _____

3. Schatz wouldn't let anyone in he thought he could give them his illness.
   _____
   _____

3 What Will You Write About? In Exercise 4, you will write a three-paragraph summary of the story "A Day's Wait." Use the "Five W's and H" questions to help you gather information, organize, and plan your essay. Remember that a summary gives only the main points of the story.

1. Who are the characters? _____

2. What happens to Schatz? _____
   _____
   _____

3. When does the story take place? _____

4. Where does the story take place? _____

5. Why does the action take place? _____
   _____
   _____

6. How does the story end? _____
   _____
   _____

4 Write a Three-Paragraph Summary. On a separate sheet of paper, write a three-paragraph summary of the story "A Day's Wait."

When you write, remember to:

1. Prewrite: Review the main points that you wrote. Do you need to add any details so that your summary will be clear and interesting to the reader? You can't use a great many details in a summary, but you need to tell the story clearly, and this means using some details.

2. Paragraph 1, Introduction: Begin with your topic sentence. Include the title and author of the short story in this paragraph. Identify the main character and what he is doing.

3. Paragraph 2, Body: Tell the main points of the story. Write at least one sentence to explain each main point. Use transitions that show time order to move the retelling of the story along.

4. Paragraph 3, Conclusion: In one or two sentences, tell what you wrote about. Don't put in your own opinion because in a summary you only retell the story. You don't give your own point of view.

5. Check spelling and capitalization.

Lesson 15

Lesson 16

1 Try Your Hand at Using Details. Write at least two sentences about each idea from the reading "The Last Leaf" listed below.

1. friendship: _____
   _____
   _____

2. the will to live: _____
   _____
   _____

3. helping others: _____
   _____
   _____

2 Use Pronouns in Sentences. Choose the correct pronouns from the lists in the box. Then rewrite each sentence, and add a sentence to it to continue the thought.

> - Personal pronouns take the place of the name of persons, places, and things: *I, we, you, he, she, it,* and *they* are used as subjects of sentences and clauses. *Me, him, her,* and *them* may be used as objects of verbs or prepositions.
> - The relative pronouns *who, whom, what, which, whose,* and *that* introduce subordinate clauses that refer to a noun or pronoun in the main clause.
> - The interrogative pronouns *who, whose, whom, what,* and *which* are used to ask questions.

1. _____ happens to Johnsy is not _____ she expects. _____
   _____
   _____

2. Behrman _____ lives downstairs decides to help Johnsy _____ he likes. _____
   _____

3. The ending was a surprise to _____, but I missed the clues _____ were there. _____
   _____
   _____

3 What Will You Write About? In Exercise 4, you will write a three-paragraph expository essay explaining how the final ivy leaf affects either Johnsy or Behrman. To help you decide which character to write about, create a cause-and-effect chain like the one below. Complete it with information from the short story about how each character is affected by the ivy leaf. You need at least three ideas to write about.

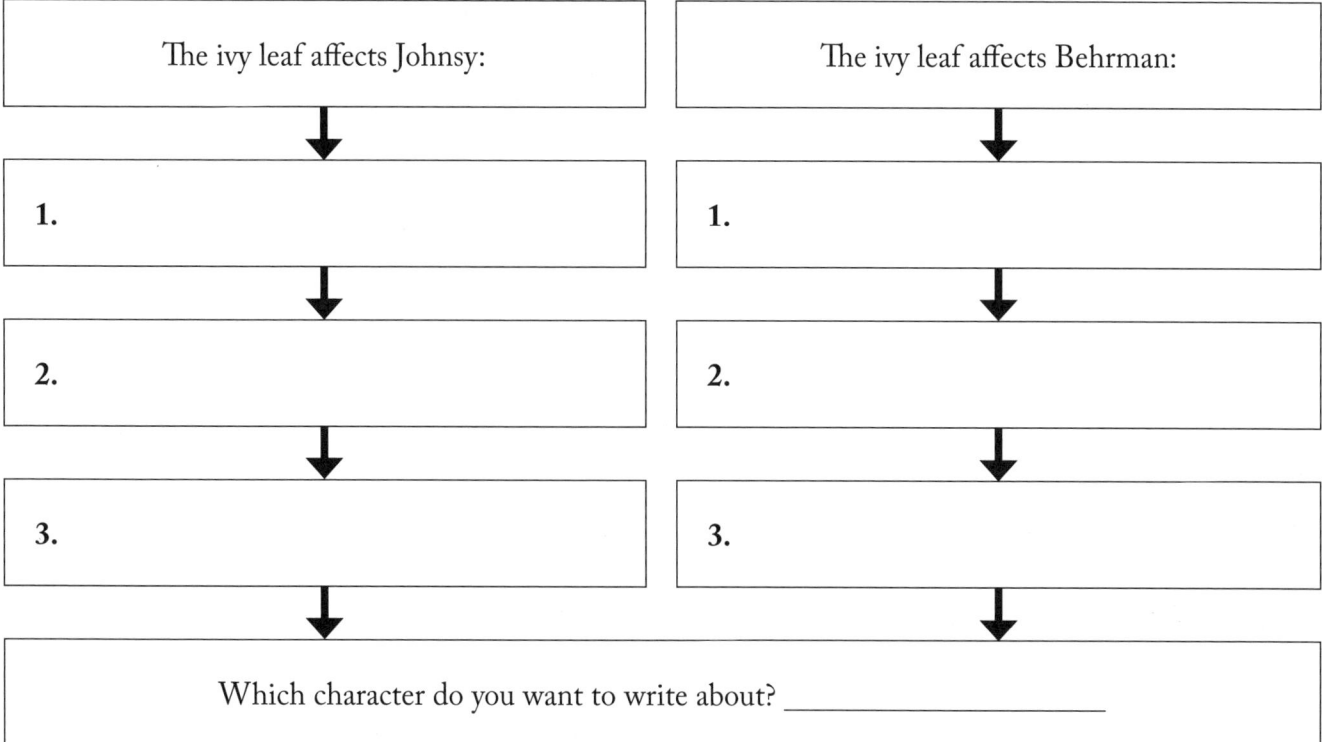

4 Write a Three-Paragraph Expository Essay. On a separate sheet of paper, write a three-paragraph expository essay explaining how the final ivy leaf affects either Johnsy or Behrman.

When you write, remember to:

1. Prewrite: Review the cause-and-effect chains and your decision about which character to write about. Do you have enough ideas and strong enough ideas about that character? If not, go back and add information.

2. Paragraph 1, Introduction: Tell what you are going to write about. The end result of the ivy leaf on the character's life is your topic sentence. Include the title and author of the short story in this paragraph. You will also need to explain who the character is.

3. Paragraph 2, Body: Develop the chain of causes and effects that affect the character you chose to write about. To connect ideas, use transitions that show cause and effect.

4. Paragraph 3, Conclusion: Restate your topic sentence, but in other words. Tie up the ideas in the essay with a sentence such as "It's too bad that Behrman did not live to see the effect of his masterpiece," or "I wonder how Johnsy reacted to the news of Behrman's masterpiece."

5. Reread your essay. Is there any place where you should add details? Also, check spelling and capitalization.

Lesson 17

1 Try Your Hand at Using Details. Write at least two sentences about each idea from "Araby" (from *The Dubliners*) listed below.

1. first love: _____
   _____
   _____

2. an unkept promise: _____
   _____
   _____

3. disappointment: _____
   _____
   _____

2 Use Pronouns in Sentences. Write the correct pronoun in each sentence. Then rewrite the sentence on the lines below, and add a sentence after it to continue the idea.

1. The narrator _____ lives with his aunt and uncle has a crush on a girl _____ we only know as Mangan's sister.
   _____
   _____

2. Not very much happens in the story, _____ is set in Dublin, Ireland, in the early 1900s.
   _____
   _____

3. If the story continued, I wonder _____ would happen next.
   _____
   _____

3 What Will You Write About? In Exercise 4, you will write a three-paragraph essay explaining whether Joyce's portrait of a teenage boy with a crush on a girl is accurate. To help you decide, list details from the story that describe how the narrator acts toward Mangan's sister.

1. _____
2. _____
3. _____
4. _____
5. _____
6. _____

Now read each detail, and cross out any that you think aren't accurate. What is your opinion of Joyce's description of the narrator? Circle one.   Accurate   Not Accurate

4 Write a Three-Paragraph Expository Essay. On a separate sheet of paper, write a three-paragraph essay to answer the question: Is James Joyce's portrait of a teenage boy with a crush on a girl accurate or not? Explain.

When you write, remember to:

1. Prewrite: Reread your list of ideas and your opinion. Choose the best three ideas to use for your essay. If you think that you have more than three good ideas, use them all.

2. Paragraph 1, Introduction: Use your opinion as your topic sentence. Include in this paragraph the title and author of the short story. Set the scene for the essay by writing a sentence or two to identify the narrator and the character on whom he has a crush.

3. Paragraph 2, Body: Develop your ideas. Use transitions that add information to connect ideas.

4. Paragraph 3, Conclusion: Restate your opinion. List the reasons that you think Joyce's portrait is or is not accurate. End with a sentence such as "The narrator would fit right in in high school today," or "The narrator would be lost in today's dating scene."

5. Reread your essay. Is there any place where you should add details? Also, check spelling and capitalization.

Lesson 18

1 Try Your Hand at Using Details. Write at least two sentences about each idea from the story "To Have or to Be" listed below.

1. a thing that you want very much: _____
   _____
   _____

2. an opinion that is very important to you: _____
   _____
   _____

3. being open-minded about new ideas: _____
   _____
   _____

2 Untangle the Confusion. Revise the sentences below so that they are clearer.

> In the hurry to get ideas down on paper, writers sometimes tangle up their ideas. Phrases end up in places that lead to misunderstanding.
>
> The photographer asked Ray in his hurry to finish to blow out the candles before they were lit.
>
> **In his hurry to finish,** the photographer asked Ray to blow out the candles before they were lit.

1. Getting credit for ideas, according to the article's writer, is important to a having-individual.
   _____
   _____

2. This idea of "having" confused me when I started to read the article as something to do with private property.
   _____
   _____

3. Material rewards are not necessarily in their work roles the only way to encourage people.
   _____
   _____

4. Review the last essay that you wrote. Revise any sentence in which a phrase or phrases are placed so that the meaning of the sentence is unclear.

_____
_____

3 What Will You Write About? In Exercise 4, you will write a three-paragraph essay to answer the question: Do you agree with the author of "To Have or to Be" that the *having* mode of existence produces the desire for power? Explain your answer using your own experience.

- State your opinion: _____

- Brainstorm a list of at least six ideas and examples from your own experience that you could use to build your essay. Use a separate sheet of paper if you need more space.

1. _____
2. _____
3. _____
4. _____
5. _____
6. _____

4 Write a Three-Paragraph Expository Essay. On a separate sheet of paper, write a three-paragraph expository essay to answer the question: Do you agree with the author of "To Have or to Be" that the *having* mode of existence produces the desire for power? Explain your answer using your own experience.

When you write, remember to:

1. Prewrite: Reread your brainstormed ideas. Choose the best ideas and examples for your essay. You can use more than three, but you need at least three.

2. Paragraph 1, Introduction: State the author's opinion. Include in the sentence the title of the reading. Then state whether you agree with the author's opinion or not. This is your topic sentence, and it may be somewhere in the paragraph besides the first sentence. List the three reasons you agree or disagree with him or her.

3. Paragraph 2, Body: Develop your ideas. Use transitions that add information or that show cause and effect to connect your ideas.

4. Paragraph 3, Conclusion: Restate your agreement or disagreement with the author's opinion. Briefly restate your reasons. Write a sentence that will tie up your ideas.

5. Reread your essay. Is there any place where you should add details? Also, check spelling and capitalization.

Lesson 18   39

Lesson 19

1 Try Your Hand at Using Details. Write at least two sentences about each idea from the play "The Woman Who Willed a Miracle: Part I" listed below.

1. taking care of someone who is sick: _____
   _____
   _____

2. being taken care of when you are ill: _____
   _____
   _____

3. learning something new: _____
   _____
   _____

2 Untangle the Confusion. Revise the sentences below to include the missing words. Each sentence has one missing word.

> Sometimes in trying to get ideas down on paper quickly, a writer will forget a word or two. That leads to confusion when writers don't proofread their work carefully.
>
> I think you're seeing what want to see.
> I think you're seeing what **you** want to see.

1. Doctors didn't give long to live because of his size and his cerebral palsy.
   _____
   _____

2. The narrator was helpful me in figuring out what was going on.
   _____
   _____

3. I was worried about what the belt for when the narrator started talking about it.
   _____
   _____

3 What Will You Write About? In Exercise 4, you will write a five-paragraph essay to describe May. Writing a five-paragraph essay is the same as writing a three-paragraph essay, but you get to use more details to develop ideas.

- First, on a separate sheet of paper, brainstorm ideas about May's personality traits. Think of as many as you can, but you need at least three.

- Second, choose three to write about. Select the ones that you think will be easiest to describe using evidence from the story.

- Third, on a separate sheet of paper, create a map like the one below. Write one personality trait in each box in the second row. In the lines coming out from each box, add details to help you explain that personality trait.

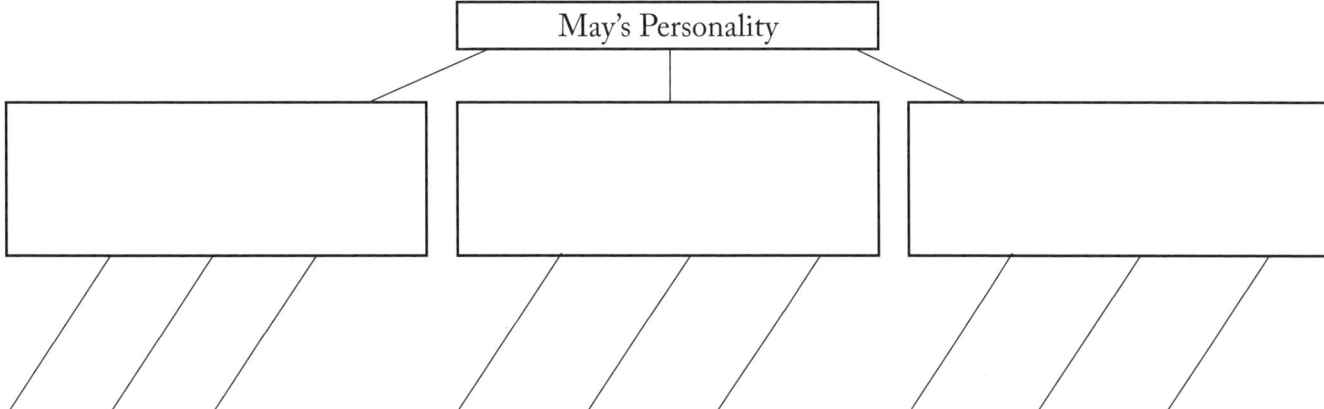

4 Write a Five-Paragraph Descriptive Essay. On a separate sheet of paper, write a five-paragraph essay to describe May.

When you write, remember to:

1. Prewrite: Review your brainstormed ideas and your idea map. Are you satisfied with what you have chosen to write about? Do you have enough details? If not, this is the time to make changes.

2. Paragraph 1, Introduction: Write your topic sentence. Identify who May is. List the three personality traits that you will write about. Include the title of the play and the playwright.

3. Paragraph 2, Body: State the first personality trait. Use details from the map to build this paragraph. Use transitions that add information to connect ideas.

4. Paragraph 3, Body: State the second personality trait. Use details to build this paragraph. Use transitions that add information.

5. Paragraph 4, Body: State the third personality trait. Use details to build this paragraph. Use transitions that add information.

6. Paragraph 5, Conclusion: Restate your topic sentence and the three personality traits. Tie up your ideas with your opinion about May.

7. Reread your essay. Is there any place where you should add details? Also, check spelling and capitalization.

Lesson 20

1 Try Your Hand at Using Details. Write at least two sentences about each idea from the play "The Woman Who Willed a Miracle: Part II" listed below.

1. a talent that you have: _____
   _____
   _____

2. a person who has overcome great difficulties: _____
   _____
   _____

3. learning something new: _____
   _____
   _____

2 Untangle the Confusion. Revise the sentences below so that they are clearer.

> In addition to misplaced phrases and omitted words, pronouns used as antecedents can confuse readers. An antecedent is a word that refers to another word in the same sentence or a nearby sentence.
>
> May was upset when the boy called Leslie a name and she went to talk to him.
>
> Did May go to talk to Leslie or to the boy? It's difficult to tell from the sentence.

1. Jason and Liam were reading the story and it made him think of Anna's brother.
   _____
   _____

2. Gladys said to May that she had made a mistake with Leslie.
   _____
   _____

3. The doctor saw Leslie regularly, but offered little hope. He gave Joe some advice early on about a home for him.
   _____
   _____

3 What Will You Write About? In Exercise 4, you will write a five-paragraph essay to explain how Leslie changed in the play "The Woman Who Willed a Miracle: Part II."

- First, reread the story and list the major changes in Leslie.
- Then, choose the three changes that you think are the most important ones. Why three? You have to write a five-paragraph essay and you can develop one change in each of the three paragraphs in the body of the essay.
- Finally, on a separate sheet of paper, create a chart like the one below to gather information and organize your ideas. Be sure to list three changes and at least three details for each.

Changes	Details
1.	1. 2. 3.

4 Write a Five-Paragraph Expository Essay. On a separate sheet of paper, write a five-paragraph essay to explain how Leslie changed in the play "The Woman Who Willed a Miracle: Part II."

When you write, remember to:

1. Prewrite: Review your list and your chart. Are you satisfied with what you have chosen to write about? Do you have enough details? If not, this is the time to make changes.
2. Paragraph 1, Introduction: Write your topic sentence. Identify who Leslie is. List the three changes that you will write about. Include the title of the play and the playwright.
3. Paragraph 2, Body: State the first change. Use details about this change to build the paragraph. Use transitions that add information to connect ideas.
4. Paragraph 3, Body: State the second change. Use details to build this paragraph. Use transitions that add information.
5. Paragraph 4, Body: State the third change. Use details to build this paragraph. Use transitions that add information.
6. Paragraph 5, Conclusion: Restate your topic sentence and the three changes. Tie up your ideas with your opinion about Leslie's development.
7. Reread your essay. Is there any place where you should add details? Also, check spelling and capitalization.

Review

1 Brainstorm Descriptive Words and Phrases to Write About. Choose one of the stories from the student book to write about.

- Write the title and the author on the first line below.
- Then write the names of two characters in the story.
- Brainstorm at least six words or phrases to describe each character.

Title and author: _____

Character 1: _____	Character 2: _____
1. _____	1. _____
2. _____	2. _____
3. _____	3. _____
4. _____	4. _____
5. _____	5. _____
6. _____	6. _____

2 Use Descriptive Words and Phrases in Sentences. Use the words and phrases from Exercise 1 above to write three sentences about each of the two characters you chose.

Character 1: _____

1. _____
   _____

2. _____
   _____

3. _____
   _____

Character 2: _____

   1. _____

   2. _____

   3. _____

3 What Will You Write About? In this book, you learned seven tools to help you gather information and organize your ideas before you write. List those seven tools below.

1. _____

2. _____

3. _____

4. _____

5. _____

6. _____

7. _____

4 What Will You Write About? From the list that you wrote in Exercise 3, choose the best tool to help you gather information and organize your ideas for each task listed below. You have done each task as you completed assignments in this book.

1. an essay that compares and contrasts two people: _____

2. an essay that explains how one person's actions affected another person: _____

3. a summary of a story or scene from a play: _____

4. a summary of an article: _____

5. trying to decide what to write about: _____

6. identifying character traits: _____

7. putting details into categories: _____

Review

5 Connect Ideas. List the four kinds of transitions that you used in this book.

1. _____
2. _____
3. _____
4. _____

6 Write a Three-Paragraph Summary. On a separate sheet of paper, write a three-paragraph summary of the scene from *On Golden Pond* that you read in Lesson 13 of the student book. Answer the "Five W's and H" questions first to gather information and organize your ideas.

7 Write a Four-Paragraph Expository Essay. On a separate sheet of paper, write a four-paragraph essay that compares two people that you know. It can be any two that have more similarities than differences. First, brainstorm people whom you might want to write about. Then choose two. Lastly, create a T-chart to list their similarities.

8 Write a Three-Paragraph Persuasive Essay. On a separate sheet of paper, write a three-paragraph essay to persuade a friend to send a donation to an organization that provides jobs to people with cerebral palsy. First, brainstorm ideas. Then, choose the best three reasons to build your essay around. You will need to create a chart to list the three reasons and then add details to explain each reason.

After you have finished each writing assignment, review the grammar and punctuation rules on the next page. Then reread what you wrote.

- Correct any problems that you find.
- Add transitions to connect ideas.
- Make a clean copy of each essay.

Some Rules to Help You Avoid Common Writing Problems

Sentence Combining

- A comma by itself can't combine parts of a sentence. Use a conjunction such as *and, but, or, nor, so, yet* and a comma to combine sentences.

- Use a comma after the first clause in a sentence that is introduced by conjunctions such as *after, although, though, because, before, if, since,* and *when.*

- If *after, although, though, because, before, if, since,* or *when* is used to begin a clause that is not the first clause in a sentence, a comma is not needed before the clause.

- Clauses need a comma and a conjunction to combine them into one sentence. Or they can be split into two sentences with a period at the end of each.

- A sentence must have a subject and a verb. Without either one, there is no sentence.

Transitions

- Transitions connect one idea to another and make it easier to see how ideas are related.

- Transitions that show time order are *after, after a while, afterward, at last, at once, before, during, finally, last, later, next, now, right away, soon, then,* and *first, second, third,* etc.

- Transitions that add information are *along with, also, another, as well as, besides, finally, for example, in addition, last, next,* and *first, second, third,* etc.

- The transitions *as a result, because, because of, consequently, on account of, so,* and *then* connect causes with their effects.

- Transitions that show similarities and differences include the following:
  Comparison: *as well as, both, in common, in comparison, like, same, similar, too*
  Differences: *although, but, however, in contrast, instead, on the other hand, unlike, yet*

Sentences

- Sentences including questions begin with capital letters.

- A period (.) is used at the end of sentences.

- A question mark (?) ends a question.

- An exclamation point (!) is used at the end of a sentence that shows strong emotion.

Pronouns

- Personal pronouns take the place of proper nouns. *I, we, you, he, she, it,* and *they* are used as subjects of sentences and clauses. *Me, him, her,* and *them* may be used as objects of verbs or prepositions.

- The relative pronouns *who, whom, which, whose,* and *that* introduce subordinate clauses that refer to a noun or pronoun in the main clause. *Who* is always used as the subject of the subordinate clause, and *whom* is always used as the object of the subordinate clause or of a preposition in the subordinate clause. *Who* and *whom* always refer to people.

- The interrogative pronouns *who, whose, whom, what,* and *which* are used to ask questions. *Who* and *whom* are used to ask about people. *Who* is always used as the subject of the verb, and *whom* is always used as the object of the verb or a preposition.